W9-CAW-477

Ronald Reagan

From Silver Screen to Oval Office

By the Editors of TIME FOR KIDS
WITH DENISE LEWIS PATRICK

HarperCollins*Publishers*

About the Author: "Reading has always been as great a passion for me as writing is," says Denise Lewis Patrick, a native of Natchitoches, Louisiana. Author of more than twenty-five books for young people, she lives in New Jersey with her husband and their four sons.

Library of Congress Cataloging-in-Publication Data is available.
ISBN 0-06-057626-X (pbk.) — ISBN 0-06-057627-8 (trade)

3 4 5 6 7 8 9 10
First Edition

Copyright © by Time Inc.

TIME For Kids and the Red Border Design are Trademarks of Time Inc. used under license.

Photography and Illustration Credits:
Cover: Michael Evans–ZUMA Press; cover inset: royalty free–Getty Images; cover flap: Ronald Reagan Presidential Library; title page: Everett Collection; contents page: Time Life Pictures–Getty Images; p.iv: AP Photo; p.1: Time Life Pictures; p.2: AP Photo–Ron Edmonds; p.3: AP Photo; p.4: Time Life Pictures; p.5: AP Photo; p.6: AP Photo; pp.6–7: AP Photo; p.8: Ronald Reagan Presidential Library; p.9: AP Photo; p.10: Ronald Reagan Presidential Library; p.11: Ronald Reagan Presidential Library; p.12: Ronald Reagan Presidential Library; p.13: AP Photo; p.14: AP Photo; p.15: Photodisc; p.16: Lou Valentino Collection; p.17: AP Photo; p.18: Ronald Reagan Presidential Library; p.19: courtesy Universal International Pictures; p.20: AP Photo; p.21: Ken James–Corbis; p.22: AP Photo; p.23: Bob Rowan–Corbis; p.24: Bettmann–Corbis; p.25: AP Photo; p.26: Ronald Reagan Presidential Library; p.27: Bettmann–Corbis; p.28: Ronald Reagan Presidential Library; p.29: Ronald Reagan Presidential Library; p.30 (top): Ronald Reagan Presidential Library; p.30 (bottom): Ronald Reagan Presidential Library; p.31: Ronald Reagan Presidential Library; p.32: Bettman–Corbis; p.33: Ronald Reagan Presidential Library; p.34: Ronald Reagan Presidential Library; p.35: Ronald Reagan Presidential Library; p.36: royalty free–Getty Images; p.37: Ronald Reagan Presidential Library; p.38: AP Photo–Ron Edmonds; p.39: Ronald Reagan Presidential Library; p.40: AP Photo–Joe Cavaretta; pp.40–41: AP Photo–Stephan Savoia; p.41: Michael Evans–Corbis; p.42: Rich Frishman; p.43 (top): Ron Chapple–Getty Images; p.43 (bottom): Reuters–Corbis; p.44 (top): Everett Collection; p.44 (middle): AP Photo–Ford Motor Company; p.44 (middle): AP Photo–Neil Armstrong/NASA; p.44 (bottom): AP Photo–Eric Risberg; back cover: Time Life Pictures–Getty Images

Acknowledgments:
For TIME For Kids: Editorial Director: Keith Garton; Editor: Jonathan Rosenbloom; Art Director: Rachel Smith; Designer: Michele Weisman; Photography Editor: Sandy Perez

 Find out more at www.timeforkids.com/bio/reagan

Contents

CHAPTER 1 **Any Child in America** 1

CHAPTER 2 **Young Dutch Grows Up** 4

CHAPTER 3 **Dutch Goes to College** 10

CHAPTER 4 **Hooray for Hollywood!** 16

CHAPTER 5 **From Statehouse to White House** . . . 22

CHAPTER 6 **The Reagans Go to Washington** 28

CHAPTER 7 **Reagan's Next Four Years** 34

CHAPTER 8 **Heading into the Sunset** 38

INTERVIEW **Talking About Ronald** 42

TIME LINE **Ronald Reagan's Key Dates** 44

"There are no great limits to growth because there are no limits of human intelligence, imagination, and wonder."

—RONALD REAGAN

▲ THOUSANDS OF PEOPLE watched Ronald Reagan being sworn in as President on January 20, 1981. Ronald's wife, Nancy, was front and center for the ceremony.

Chapter 1

Any Child in America

The winter day was icy cold, and the skies over Washington, D.C., surely were going to fill with snow. The weather had been so much warmer and sunnier at the California ranch Ronald and Nancy Reagan left behind!

But the Reagans were excited as their dark limousine pulled up to the beautiful White House. On that day, January 20, 1981, Ronald Wilson Reagan had just been sworn in as the fortieth President of the United States.

The new President held hands with his wife as they passed through the famous rooms. There

▲ *TIME* MAGAZINE featured Reagan on its 1980 cover. It was issued just after he was elected President.

▲ A SNOW-COVERED lawn welcomed the Reagans to the White House.

was the elegant East Room, where large parties and dinners were held. Then came the Oval Office, where other Presidents had worked before him. At last he and Nancy entered the family rooms. This is where the Reagans would live for at least the next four years.

As a boy Reagan had once lived in an apartment over the store where his father worked. There wasn't a lot of extra spending money when he was growing up.

Like many kids, he dreamed about being wealthy, successful, and famous. Finally his dreams had come true.

President Reagan later said, "If I could do this, then truly any child in America had an opportunity to do it."

He had been an athlete, a radio announcer, a movie actor, a union leader, and a state governor. Now he was seventy years old—the oldest person ever elected President. When many people were retiring, Reagan was beginning the most important job of his life. Could he lead a nation?

Ronald Reagan had been elected at a time when many Americans were struggling because they had lost jobs. Many thought the United States was less powerful than it had been. Reagan believed Americans had forgotten their dreams— for themselves and their nation. He was ready to help his country remember how to dream.

▲ **RONALD WAS BORN** in this apartment above a store in Tampico, Illinois.

Chapter 2

Young Dutch Grows Up

Jack Reagan smiled when his son Ronald was born at home on February 6, 1911. "He looks like a fat little Dutchman," he said. "But who knows, he might grow up to be President someday!"

Ronald's mother, Nelle, was happy that their son was healthy. But when two-year-old Neil saw his baby brother, he was disappointed. He'd wanted a sister!

◄ **BABY RONNIE** was a few months old when this picture was taken.

Although Dutch was born in Tampico, Illinois, the Reagan family moved many times when the boys were young. Jack sold shoes, but he was fired from jobs because he had a problem with drinking too much. Nelle explained to the boys that their father had a sickness, and that he was trying to get better. Jack never quite recovered from his alcoholism. Over the years the family had some hard times because of that. Yet Ronald still remembered his father as charming, easygoing, and a wonderful storyteller.

Nelle stayed at home, taking care of the children. Sometimes she sewed clothes or worked with Jack to make extra money. She was very religious and expected her sons to pray and to attend church. Nelle also told them to believe in their dreams.

Hello, Dixon

The Reagans finally settled in Dixon, Illinois, in 1920. Going to so many different schools hadn't been easy for the Reagan boys. At first shy Dutch didn't make new friends as quickly as his more outgoing brother did. Neil, who was called Moon by the family, was a better athlete.

▲ HOME, SWEET HOME!
In 1920 the Reagans moved to this neat house in Dixon, Illinois.

Dutch spent a lot of time reading—including a book about wolves that he especially loved—but he still enjoyed sports very much. He played his first football game with Moon and some friends when he was nine years old. Although he wasn't very good at the sport, he was hooked. He also ice-skated and swam. Soon skinny

little Dutch became an excellent swimmer.

Besides playing sports, Dutch and Moon had fun in other ways. Sometimes, when the boys had a few nickels, they would go to the movies. On many evenings Nelle would make popcorn and read the boys stories. She loved poems and plays, and she performed at schools and churches in nearby towns. Nelle tried to get her sons to join her. When Dutch was about ten, he memorized a speech and then recited it during a show. The audience applauded. He didn't know it yet, but that stage experience would play an important part in his life.

Dutch had another memorable experience, which got him into trouble. One July Fourth, when he was eleven, he bought some illegal fireworks and set them off near the town's bridge. A police officer took him to the station, where his father paid the $14.50 fine. Dutch had to work hard to pay back his father.

◄ DUTCH LIKED TO PLAY football. He is second from the left in this picture. Check out the uniforms!

Dutch the Teenager

When Dutch and Moon became teenagers, they looked for summer jobs to help out their family. They did odd jobs for the Ringling Brothers Circus. Dutch also worked on a building construction crew. The hard work carrying bricks made him strong. His body filled out, and he had muscles!

When Dutch was fifteen, he got a job as a lifeguard at Lowell Park Beach. Dutch was popular there. Everyone at the beach could pick him out from the crowd, with his broad shoulders and shiny dark hair. Dutch worked seven days a week, twelve hours a day. He was an excellent lifeguard and worked hard at this important job. During seven summers there, he rescued seventy-seven people.

At Dixon High School he made

◀ DUTCH was a hard-working and popular teenager.

good grades but only won a spot on the second-string football team. Dutch was

▲ DUTCH JOINED THE DRAMA Club in high school. He is the fourth person from the left, performing in a play called *Captain Applejack*.

disappointed, since he loved the sport. He was stubborn, though, and he didn't give up. His determination got him a spot as right guard on the first team for his senior year.

He also discovered something new in high school—acting. Margaret Cleaver, a girl Dutch liked, was in the drama club at Dixon High. Dutch joined, too. Dutch also knew Margaret was planning to go to college after she graduated. Not many people from Dixon went to college. No one in Dutch's family had gone.

Nelle encouraged both her sons to apply to college. Moon wasn't interested, but Dutch was. He figured he could play football there, and he could see Margaret all the time. He only had to figure out how to earn the money he needed to pay for his education.

Chapter 3

Dutch Goes to College

After Dutch graduated from high school in 1928, he went to Eureka College—the same school Margaret was attending—in the tiny town of Eureka, Illinois. Dutch talked to a few people at the college and got a football scholarship that covered his school fees. To pay for his books and his room, he got a job as a waiter in the school dining room.

Dutch was not as good at football as many of his

◄ **DUTCH WARMS UP** before a college football game.

teammates. But he *was* good at acting. When Dutch wasn't playing ball, he took part in the drama group with Margaret. He loved speaking in public, and he loved the reactions of an audience. But Dutch enjoyed acting wherever he was. Using a broom handle as a microphone in his room, he would perform exciting play-by-play "shows" of pretend athletic events. Secretly he dreamed of becoming a radio sports announcer once he finished college.

Dutch was at Eureka College in 1929 when the Great Depression began. The entire country had money problems. Businesses had to close, and people lost their jobs and their homes. Many could not afford new clothes or food. The depression lasted for several years. During the summers, Dutch was able to work at his old lifeguard job. Yet money for school was still tight. He considered dropping out, but Dutch Reagan was not a quitter. He found work on campus as a dishwasher in the girls' dorm, and he stayed in school.

Get a Job

Dutch graduated from Eureka in 1932 with a degree in economics. His father wanted him to get a sales job in a store, but Dutch decided to follow his own mind. So he borrowed his father's old car and drove to Chicago to try to find the job he really wanted—in radio. All the big stations were looking for

▲ RADIO DAYS! Dutch's first job out of college was as a radio announcer.

someone with a lot of experience. But there was a tiny station in Davenport, Iowa, called WOC that was willing to give him a chance.

Dutch put on one of his best "broomstick" performances. He pretended that he was calling one of the old college football games he'd played in.

He was hired! Dutch Reagan, radio reporter, read everything from local news to weather reports. After a few months WOC's sister radio station in Des Moines, Iowa, needed a sports director. Soon Dutch Reagan was traveling all over the region for WHO, announcing both college and professional sports.

Radio Days

Ronald Reagan was a sports radio announcer during the 1930s. At that time, radio was America's most popular form of entertainment. Listeners could tune in to live music and comedy shows, Westerns, space adventures, soap operas, mysteries, news broadcasts, and books read on the air.

On October 30, 1938, an actor named Orson Welles (pictured above) read a radio play called "War of the Worlds." Many listeners thought Martians were attacking Earth. People ran out of their homes screaming. Others drove their cars to safety. It wasn't until later that evening that listeners learned it was just a radio play!

Listeners tuned in to hear his smooth voice. His descriptions made the events come alive.

In the spring of 1937, he went to California with the Chicago Cubs to report on their pre-season baseball games. They played not far from Hollywood. Dutch had a friend from Iowa who now made movies there. He decided to get in touch.

His friend, Joy Hodges, suggested he find an agent to help him get into movies. He made some phone calls and met an agent who got him a screen test at Warner Brothers Studios. Dutch had to wear makeup, memorize a script, and recite his lines with another actor. All the while the movie cameras were rolling. Dutch was relaxed and loved every second of his screen test!

▶ DUTCH POSES ON THE SET
for his screen test.

You're Hired!

The studio people tried to convince him to stay in Hollywood until a decision was made. But Dutch, who had squeezed in his screen test between baseball games, had to leave. "I've got to get back to my job in Des Moines," he told his agent.

▲ THIS FAMOUS SIGN welcomed Dutch to Hollywood.

"The season opener's coming up in a few days and I've got to broadcast the Cubs' games." Reluctantly Dutch went back to Iowa the next day with the Cubs, not sure how he'd done.

Just two days later, on April 2, 1937, someone at WHO handed Dutch a telegram from his movie agent. It read: *Warners offers contract seven years ... starting $200 a week. ... What shall I do?*

Dutch wrote back immediately: *Sign before they change their minds.*

The day he left WHO, Dutch left his nickname behind. Ronald Reagan was going to Hollywood to become a movie star.

Hooray for Hollywood!

The first film Ronald Reagan made for Warner Brothers was *Love Is on the Air*. He played a radio announcer! At first Ronald was nervous. But as soon as he started speaking his lines, he relaxed.

▲ A MOVIE MAGAZINE featured Ronald Reagan and Jane Wyman.

While he was filming *Brother Rat* in 1938, he met an actress named Jane Wyman. They got married in January 1940. The next year their daughter, Maureen, was born. A few years later, they adopted a son, Michael.

The Reagans made many Hollywood friends. Most of them belonged to the Screen

Actors Guild (SAG). SAG was a union that helped actors get fair treatment from movie studios. Like most actors, Ronald had to join SAG—even though he didn't want to. But once he saw that many actors weren't getting a fair deal in Hollywood, he became active in the union. Soon he was a leader of the group.

Ronald Joins the Army

Ronald's movie career came to a halt in 1941 when he was called to serve in World War II. Every soldier had to pass a doctor's exam to fight in combat. Ronald failed the eye test, but he still had to join up. He was assigned to make training films for new soldiers.

While he was with the unit, he noticed that time and money were wasted and fewer people were needed to do the work. This idea would take him on a path far from Hollywood.

▶ RONALD JOINED the army in 1941. He is shown here with Jane and their daughter, Maureen.

When the war ended in 1945, Captain Reagan returned to Hollywood, but it was harder to get good roles. It was a rough time for him. His father had died in 1941, and Ronald needed to earn more money to care for his mother. His marriage was also in trouble, and soon he and Jane divorced.

Ronald began to spend more time with SAG. In a few years he was elected its president. He also became interested in politics. As a member of the Democratic Party, he campaigned for the party's candidates running for office in California. Later Ronald campaigned for some Republicans whose ideas he believed in.

Ronald Meets Nancy

It was around this time that Ronald met a young actress named Nancy Davis. Ronald later said, "I think my life really began when I met Nancy." They fell in love and married in 1952.

The couple had two children, Patricia and Ronald Jr. Nancy encouraged her

◄ THE BRIDE AND GROOM cut the wedding cake. It was love at first bite.

husband to get more involved with SAG. She became Ronald's closest and most trusted advisor.

In 1957 Ronald and Nancy made *Hellcats of the Navy.* It was their first and only film together. After making one more movie, Nancy decided to stay home to take care of her husband and their children.

Altogether, Ronald had starred in more than fifty movies. He still had his appealing voice and his good looks. But he hadn't had a hit movie in years, and now he was getting fewer offers.

Welcome to TV Land!

Ronald also had another job during this time. He was the host of a TV show called *GE Theater.* Ronald introduced every show and acted in a few episodes each season. He gave speeches around the country for the show's sponsor, General Electric. Ronald talked about the importance of doing things without waiting for the government to do them for you. Ronald won people over to the idea of a smaller, more efficient government.

Ronald began to think about a different kind of public life. His leadership in SAG, which lasted until 1960, made it possible for him to help its members have better working conditions. He liked meeting people and trying to make a difference in their lives. Ronald thought he might run for political office. He wanted to change the way California's government was run.

When GE ended their program in 1962, Ronald looked for something to keep him busy. He was

wealthy from his days on television. His mother had died that summer, and he thought hard about changing his life.

Ronald also changed political parties. His ideas of fewer taxes and a smaller

◄ REAGAN ENJOYED
campaigning for governor and
meeting the voters.

government were more
like those of the
Republicans than those of
the Democrats. By 1966
he felt he could be a
strong leader—better than
California's current
governor, Edmund
Brown. So, with Nancy's
support, Ronald entered
the race.

The new candidate
promised that, if elected,
he would make sure the
state did not spend so
much of its citizens'
money. He said the
government should not
make so many decisions
for the people. He
believed most Americans
wanted fewer laws to
obey and lower taxes to
pay. Ronald Reagan won
the election by almost
one million votes.

Mystery Person

☞ **CLUE 1:** From the time I was a kid in Austria, I was interested in bodybuilding. My dream came true when I moved to the United States in 1968 and won several important bodybuilding championships.

☞ **CLUE 2:** I started to appear in movies in 1976. I played myself in a documentary called *Pumping Iron*. Then I went on to play action heroes in hit movies.

☞ **CLUE 3:** Like Ronald Reagan, I decided to go into politics. In 2003 I won the election as governor of California.

Who am I?

From Statehouse to
White House

Governor Reagan was eager to begin his new job. He chose a team of advisers who shared his ideas to help him change California.

The serious issues of a state were harder to solve than problems in the movies. Most of California's lawmakers were members of the Democratic Party and didn't agree with many of Ronald's ideas. But he needed their votes to make new laws or change

◀ **RONALD REAGAN** is sworn in as the governor of California.

THE CALIFORNIA CAPITOL is located in Sacramento. Reagan had to get along with members of both political parties.

old ones. Because he didn't have any experience as an elected official, Ronald had to find ways to work with the lawmakers.

The governor had other problems to face. First he had to figure out how to save money and cut spending. So he raised taxes. He closed some state hospitals—a decision both doctors and patients fought against. He also asked state colleges to start charging students money to go to school. (Up until then California students could attend state colleges for free.)

Troubled Times

Throughout the state, angry students held protest marches. They also held "sit-ins," where hundreds of

▲ IN 1967 POLICE TRIED TO KEEP STUDENT PROTESTERS from becoming violent on the campus of the University of California, Berkeley.

people sat down in one spot, blocking public buildings or roads.

More protests broke out the following year. In 1968 African Americans in Los Angeles—and elsewhere around the United States—reacted with anger to the murder of civil rights leader Dr. Martin Luther King Jr. Homes and businesses in Watts, a mostly black area of Los Angeles, were burned and robbed. The streets became dangerous.

The riots made many Californians afraid. Governor

Reagan had to act quickly and decisively. He sent National Guard troops into Los Angeles. The next year he sent the troops armed with bayonets and tear gas onto college campuses, where students were protesting the unpopular Vietnam War. The National Guard finally ended the riots. Some people called Ronald a hero for ending the unrest. Others said he acted too forcefully and showed poor judgment by sending so many troops to stop the protests.

Passing Laws

But with peace restored, Ronald could turn to other business. He got laws passed to protect parklands in the state. He cut state spending so California had fewer money problems. He worked with lawmakers to cut taxes and help poor families. By the time Ronald's first four years as governor ended, he had learned how to get things done. People liked him because, when he talked, he made them feel comfortable. Many

▶ **CALIFORNIA LAWMAKERS** look on as Governor Reagan signs a bill into law.

Californians thought he had done a good job in moving the state forward. In 1970 Ronald ran for a second term and won.

Ronald Runs for President

The Republican Party had been watching Governor Reagan's continued success in California. In 1976 he hoped to be chosen as his party's candidate for President. He campaigned to get the nomination but lost to Gerald Ford. (Ford went on to lose the election.) So Ronald spent the next four years giving speeches around the country—keeping his name and

▲ REAGAN GAVE HIS ACCEPTANCE SPEECH for the Republican nomination for President. George H. W. Bush ran as his vice president.

his ideas before the American public.

In 1980 Ronald Reagan tried again, this time getting his party's nomination to run against President Jimmy Carter. Ronald talked about his ideas to balance the budget, cut taxes, and make the military stronger. He talked about the greatness of America's ideals and the need for a forceful leader. Ronald made strong connections with the crowds as he joked with them. He asked voters: "Are you better off now than you were four years ago?"

On Election Day they answered. Ronald Wilson Reagan beat Jimmy Carter and brought Republicans back to the White House.

Party Animals

A political party is a group of people who want to elect to office someone who agrees with their ideas.

In the United States, the two largest political parties are the Democrats and the Republicans.

In the 1870s Thomas Nast, a newspaper cartoonist, used the donkey to stand for the Democrats and the elephant to stand for the Republicans. He chose the donkey because it is strong-willed and the elephant because it is intelligent but easily controlled.

Democrats today say that the donkey is smart and brave, while Republicans say that the elephant is strong and dignified.

The Reagans Go to
Washington

A fter Ronald was sworn in to office in 1981, he and Nancy settled comfortably in their new home— the White House. All of Reagan's children, along with Moon and his wife, gathered to celebrate his

inauguration. There were dinners, dances, and lots of parties to enjoy. The Reagans looked forward to all of the great things they would be doing.

But two months later, on March 30, 1981, tragedy struck. The new President had just given a speech at a Washington hotel. As Reagan, his staff members, and his bodyguards were

▲ JUST BEFORE HE WAS SHOT, Ronald Reagan waved to a crowd of admirers.

leaving, four gunshots suddenly rang out. The President was hit. So were Press Secretary James Brady, a Secret Service agent, and a police officer. All of the men were rushed to hospitals.

Reagan needed emergency surgery. Before he was operated on, he joked with the doctor: "I sure hope you're a Republican." Even while wounded, Reagan used his humor to relax those around him.

Within weeks the President recovered. The police arrested John Hinckley, the man who shot Reagan and the others. Doctors found that Hinckley was mentally ill. He was sent to a special hospital instead of prison.

◄ RONALD AND NANCY were surrounded by their family on inauguration night.

President Reagan
survived the attack
more determined
than ever to keep his
election promises.
As governor
President Reagan had
learned how
important it was to negotiate
with politicians who might not share his views.
Reagan and his Republican supporters were

Meet Nancy Reagan

▲ **NANCY REAGAN poses in the Red Room
of the White House.**

Nancy Reagan was born
Anne Francis Robbins on
July 6, 1921, in New York City.
Her parents nicknamed her
Nancy. Shortly after she was
born, her father left the family.
Later her mother married Dr.
Loyal Davis, who adopted
Nancy.

After college Nancy became
an actress in New York City. A
movie studio official suggested

conservative politicians. People who consider themselves conservatives don't like having too many government rules that regulate how people live and do business. They don't like too many taxes, or taxes that they consider too high or unfair.

Many Democrats are more liberal. They believe that the government can help solve more problems than Reagan thought. The Democrats want more government programs—which would mean new or higher taxes to help pay for the programs.

As President, Reagan's easy way of communicating helped him push through many conservative ideas— including a law that greatly lowered the taxes many Americans had to pay.

◄ NANCY REAGAN worked hard to make the Foster Grandparent Program a success.

she try out for films. So Nancy moved to California, where she met Ronald Reagan. "My life really began when I married my husband," she has said. The actress appeared in eleven movies before

becoming a full-time wife and mother.

As First Lady, she was active in the war against drugs and alcohol, as well as being in a foster grandparent program. Nancy redid parts of the White House. She was famous for the elegant, formal dinners that she gave for the world's leaders and for her fashionable clothes, which were often a bright shade of red.

▲ **BRITISH PRIME MINISTER** Margaret Thatcher and Ronald Reagan worked closely together and were friends. The two are walking the President's dog Lucky.

A Safer World

President Reagan also turned his attention to finding ways to make the world safer. Perhaps living through World War II made Reagan especially concerned about protecting America. He would spend more and more money to build up the U.S. armed forces. He wanted to create a space shield, called Star Wars after the popular movie, that would blow up any enemy missiles launched at the United States. But some Americans questioned the President. They felt his actions encouraged other countries, such as the Soviet Union, to build up their own armies and weapons supplies.

At the time, the Soviet Union was the strongest enemy of the United States. The nation was made up of many small countries that had been joined together after World War II. It was ruled by one central government, which made all the rules and decisions for its people. The communist system of government was very different from our democratic one, where Americans elect leaders and vote on laws. Reagan proposed that both countries reduce the number of nuclear missiles they had. The Soviet leader, Mikhail Gorbachev, agreed to talk.

Reagan knew that he needed four more years in office to reach this important goal. Americans gave him the chance in 1984 as they elected him to a second term.

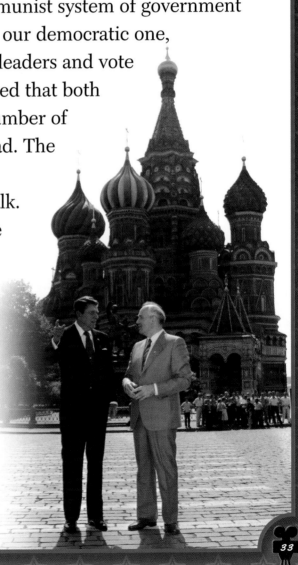

▶ RONALD REAGAN and Mikhail Gorbachev met many times. Here they are shown in Moscow.

Reagan's Next Four Years

Reagan wasted no time in getting down to the business of making the world safer. In 1985 he met with Gorbachev in Switzerland to begin their talks. The two leaders got to know each other and became

▲ **REAGAN AND GORBACHEV** helped bring about peace between their nations.

▲ ON A VISIT TO BERLIN, Reagan challenged Gorbachev to tear down the Berlin Wall.

friends. Their common goals smoothed the way for lessening the number of nuclear weapons.

During the talks, President Reagan traveled to Berlin, Germany, in 1987. This city had been divided at the end of World War II. The U.S. and its allies oversaw a free West Berlin and the Soviets controlled East Berlin. In 1961 the Russians built the Berlin Wall, cutting the city in two. Anyone trying to escape to West Berlin—and to freedom—was arrested or shot. The Berlin Wall was a symbol of the cold war—the struggle for power between the Soviet Union and the United States. The wall was a sign of the unfairness of the Soviet system.

Reagan gave a speech to the people of West Berlin that challenged Gorbachev to "tear down this wall!"

Jelly Beans, Mr. President?

Everybody has a favorite snack, and Presidents are no different from other hungry Americans. Ronald Reagan kept a jar of jelly beans on his desk. James Buchanan gave sauerkraut and mashed potato parties! Check out the foods some other Presidents raided the kitchen to find.

☞ **George Washington**
cream of peanut soup

☞ **Ulysses S. Grant**
cucumbers soaked in vinegar

☞ **Chester A. Arthur**
mutton chops

☞ **Franklin D. Roosevelt**
fried cornmeal mush

☞ **Dwight Eisenhower**
TV dinners

☞ **Bill Clinton**
burgers and fries

Making History

A little more than six months later, a historic day arrived. On December 8, 1987, Reagan and Gorbachev came to an agreement to reduce nuclear weapons. This treaty was one of the steps in the breakup of the Soviet Union. President Reagan had a political triumph. Within another two years, after Reagan left office, the Berlin Wall finally would come down.

Nearing the end of his Presidency, Reagan could look back at other events—good and bad. He had appointed the first female Supreme Court justice, Sandra Day O'Connor, in 1982. He had shown Americans that he could also feel deep sadness. When the space shuttle *Challenger* exploded in 1986, killing its crew, the President comforted the nation. He said, "The future doesn't belong to the faint-hearted. It belongs to the brave."

But the President also approved a secret and illegal sale of weapons to the Middle Eastern country of Iran. He had been trying to win the release of Americans being held hostage by Iran's ally, Lebanon. Some of the weapons money was also given to Contra rebels. They were trying to overthrow the democratically elected government of Nicaragua—a nation in Central America. Many of Reagan's aides lost their jobs because of the Iran-Contra affair, but Reagan stayed in office.

Reagan's second term ended in 1988. When he smiled and waved for the last time from the White House, he was an ordinary citizen once again— that nice guy with a great voice that people loved to listen to.

◄ FAREWELL! The President gave a good-bye salute on the day he left office. Next stop? California.

Chapter 8

Heading into the Sunset

Nancy and Ronald returned to their home in Los Angeles, California. As a retired President, experienced in national and world affairs, Reagan was comfortable as an elder statesman. He spent his time writing a book about his experiences as President and giving speeches to organizations and companies around the globe.

What most of the world didn't realize was that the former President was suffering from Alzheimer's disease.

▶ THE FORMER President continued to give speeches after he left office.

► **MAUREEN REAGAN** and her husband, Dennis, helped Nancy care for Ronald.

People with Alzheimer's slowly forget how to speak and eat. They can no longer understand what is going on around them. They can no longer recognize their family. Finally Alzheimer's patients must have someone else take care of all their needs. The disease is frightening for both patients and their loved ones.

A Journey Begins

Reagan shared news of his illness with the nation in 1994. He handwrote a letter that was sent to newspapers across the world, ending with these words:

"I now begin the journey that will lead me into the sunset of my life."

Nancy and a team of nurses and helpers spent the next ten years caring for him as he gradually became weaker. Nancy worked to increase awareness about Alzheimer's and called for more

◀ THOUSANDS of Californians wanted to say good-bye to Reagan as his body was taken to be buried.

scientific research into the disease.

On June 6, 2004, Ronald Reagan died at home. He was ninety-three. Across the country people mourned the President's death. His state funeral was held five days later at the National Cathedral in Washington, D.C. Crowding the service were friends from every part of Reagan's past—including Mikhail Gorbachev. Reagan was buried on the grounds of his presidential library in Simi Valley, California, that evening.

Many people admire Ronald Reagan for helping big business and shrinking government by getting rid of many costly programs. Others say these programs were needed by average and poor Americans.

▶ NANCY REAGAN kissed her husband's casket. They were married for fifty-two years.

But all Americans might agree that Ronald Reagan succeeded in carrying out the important mission his loyal supporters gave him long ago. He reminded people how great America could be. He helped weaken communist rule and paved the way for a freer world. These were, in the end, his finest roles.

FAMOUS QUOTES
Ronald Reagan Said It

Ronald Reagan was known for his wit and his humor, as well as for summing up a serious thought in just a few words.

"I have left orders to be awakened at any time in case of national emergency, even if I'm in a cabinet meeting."

"People don't start wars, governments do."

"Thomas Jefferson once said, 'We should never judge a President by his age, only by his works.' And ever since he told me that, I stopped worrying."

"You can tell a lot about a fellow's character by his way of eating jelly beans."

Interview

Talking About
Ronald

▲ Ron Reagan

TIME FOR KIDS editor Kathryn Hoffman Satterfield spoke with Ron Reagan about his father.

Q: *How do you think your father would want people to remember him?*
A: After he was shot, he felt even more strongly that he was President for a reason—to do good for others. He was a decent, honest person. That made him an attractive leader.

Q: *If he were alive today, what would he work on?*
A: He'd probably work on reducing taxes, improving peace in the Middle East, and dealing with terrorism.

Q: *What is your fondest memory of your father?*
A: Whether we were body surfing in the ocean or

swimming races in our backyard pool, we both loved the water. He'd often play touch football with me and my friends. He was supposed to be in his office [when he was governor of California], but he couldn't resist the fact that there was a football game going on with a bunch of seven-year-olds. So he'd play quarterback for both teams.

Q: *What do you find most inspiring about your dad?*
A: His personal decency. As President you're a powerful guy, and you can boss people around. But he never took advantage. He was always good to the people around him and treated them the same, whether they were mowing the lawn or they were his secretary of state.

Ronald Reagan's
Key Dates

1911	Born on February 6, in Tampico, Illinois
1937	Appears in his first movie, *Love Is on the Air*
1947	Elected president of the Screen Actors Guild
1948	Divorced from Jane Wyman
1952	Marries Nancy Davis
1966	Elected California's governor
1980	Elected President of the United States
1981	Shot in attempted assassination
1984	Re-elected President
2004	Dies on June 6, in Los Angeles, California

1913 The moving assembly line is introduced by Henry Ford to build cars.

1969 Neil Armstrong becomes the first person to walk on the moon.

1991 The U.S. Women's Soccer Team wins the World Cup.